TheFA.com

Printed under license by Parragon
Distributed by D.C. Thomson & Co. Ltd
185 Fleet Street
London EC4A 2HS

All information is correct at time of creation, May 2010.

ISBN 978-1-84535-436-7

Printed in UK

ENGLAND

THE OFFICIAL ENGLAND ANNUAL 2011

PLAYER PROFILES

How much do you know about your favourite England players? This section contains vital stats and facts about the best players in the country.

MANAGER

Capello has won domestic league titles with every club he has coached.

FABIO CAPELLO

On Friday 14 December 2007, the FA unveiled Fabio Capello as the England Manager.

Before becoming a manager, Fabio Capello enjoyed a successful playing career as a midfielder with Roma, Juventus and AC Milan. He also **earned 32 caps for Italy**. Somewhat ironically, he remembers his winning goal against England at Wembley in 1973 as the **highlight of his playing career**.

His **16-year managerial career** has encompassed spells at AC Milan, Real Madrid, AS Roma and Juventus. In total, Capello has **won nine League titles** in Italy and Spain as well as lifting the **European Cup with AC Milan in 1994**.

He began his coaching career with AC Milan, and graduated to take charge of the first team in 1991. He brought huge success to the club, winning four Serie A titles in five seasons and overseeing European Cup success with a 4-0 Final victory over Barcelona in 1994. A season at Real Madrid followed where the team won La Liga. After a brief return to AC Milan, Capello joined Roma. The Serie A title was secured in 2001 and Capello was recruited by Juventus in 2004 where he won Serie A in both 2005 and 2006. Capello returned to Real Madrid for the 2006–2007 campaign and achieved what their five previous managers could not, he led them to the La Liga title once again.

ENGLAND MANAGER STATS
DATE OF BIRTH 18.06.1946
PLACE OF BIRTH Gorizia, Italy
MANAGED 22
WON 16
LOST 4
DRAWN 2
GOALS 56

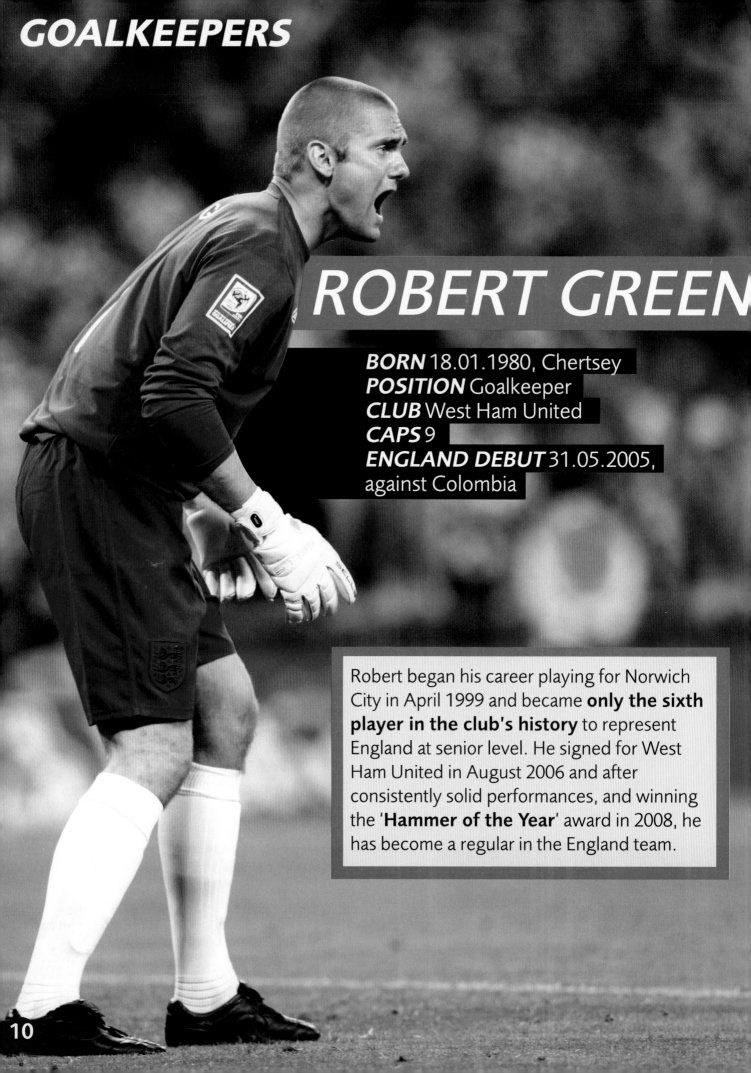

ROBERT GREEN

BORN 18.01.1980, Chertsey
POSITION Goalkeeper
CLUB West Ham United
CAPS 9
ENGLAND DEBUT 31.05.2005, against Colombia

Robert began his career playing for Norwich City in April 1999 and became **only the sixth player in the club's history** to represent England at senior level. He signed for West Ham United in August 2006 and after consistently solid performances, and winning the '**Hammer of the Year**' award in 2008, he has become a regular in the England team.

DAVID JAMES

BORN 01.08.1970, Welwyn Garden City
POSITION Goalkeeper
CLUB Portsmouth
CAPS 49
ENGLAND DEBUT 29.03.1997, against Mexico

International Friendly
England v Egypt
Wembley Stadium – London
03.03.2010

David won his first senior England cap against Mexico in 1997 and his excellent goalkeeping skills helped England qualify for Euro 2004. In April 2007 James **broke the record for the most clean sheets** in Premier League history. On 14 February 2009, James achieved the all-time Premier League record for appearances and has played over **560 Premier League games**.

JOE HART

BORN 19.04.1987, Shrewsbury
POSITION Goalkeeper
CLUB Manchester City
CAPS 1
ENGLAND DEBUT 01.06.2008, against Trinidad & Tobago

Under-21 International Friendly
England v Azerbaijan
StadiumMK, Milton Keynes
08.06.2009

At only 21 years and 43 days old and after 12 appearances at Under-21 level, Manchester City goalkeeper Joe Hart made his **debut** for the England senior team. Hart was a second-half substitute for David James in England's friendly against Trinidad & Tobago in June 2008, where he earned his **first senior cap**.

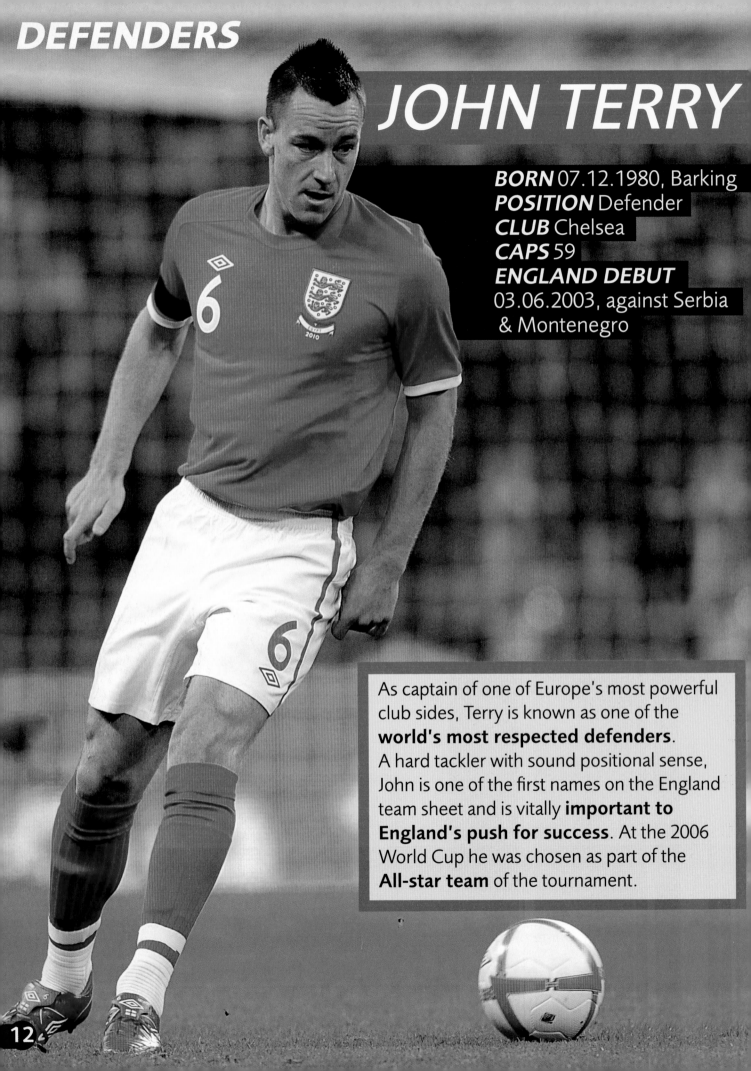

JOHN TERRY

BORN 07.12.1980, Barking
POSITION Defender
CLUB Chelsea
CAPS 59
ENGLAND DEBUT
03.06.2003, against Serbia
& Montenegro

As captain of one of Europe's most powerful club sides, Terry is known as one of the **world's most respected defenders**. A hard tackler with sound positional sense, John is one of the first names on the England team sheet and is vitally **important to England's push for success**. At the 2006 World Cup he was chosen as part of the **All-star team** of the tournament.

12

MATTHEW UPSON

BORN 18.04.1979, Hartismere
POSITION Defender
CLUB West Ham United
CAPS 19
ENGLAND DEBUT 22.05.2003,
against South Africa

*International Friendly
England v Egypt
Wembley Stadium – London
03.03.2010*

Upson's **impressive performances** with previous club Birmingham City led to an international call-up in May 2003 to face South Africa. In 2008, he firmly established his place at **the heart of England's defence**, featuring in the last four internationals of the year. Upson scored his **first international goal** against Germany in November 2008.

LEIGHTON BAINES

BORN 11.12.1984, Kirkby
POSITION Defender
CLUB Everton
CAPS 1
ENGLAND DEBUT 03.03.2010,
against Egypt

*International Friendly
England v Egypt
Wembley Stadium – London
03.03.2010*

A **set-piece specialist**, Leighton Baines started his career with Wigan Athletic in 2002 in Division 2, where he was part of the **Championship-winning** team. Two seasons later they earned promotion to the Premier League. Baines was in high demand before he chose to sign for Everton, where he has mastered the art of being an **attacking full-back**.

RIO FERDINAND

BORN 07.11.1978, Peckham
POSITION Defender
CLUB Manchester United
CAPS 76
ENGLAND DEBUT 15.11.1997,
against Cameroon

Coming through the Youth Academy of West Ham United, Ferdinand developed a unique composure and style of play. His **commanding performances** for England at the 2002 World Cup cemented his status as one of the **world's best defenders**. He made eight England appearances throughout 2008 and **is often called upon to captain the side**.

FRANK LAMPARD

BORN 20.06.1978, Romford
POSITION Midfielder
CLUB Chelsea
CAPS 77
ENGLAND DEBUT
10.10.1999, against Belgium

The son of former West Ham United and England full-back, Frank Lampard Senior, Lampard broke into the Hammers' first team at just 17 years old. Frank's **passing and movement** make him one of the best midfielders in the world. For Chelsea, he has scored **more than 20 goals** in each of the last five seasons and is their third **highest all-time scorer.** He had the honour of scoring England's 500th goal at Wembley Stadium.

GARETH BARRY

International Friendly
England v Egypt
Wembley Stadium – London
03.03.2010

BORN 23.02.1981, Hastings
POSITION Midfielder
CLUB Manchester City
CAPS 36
ENGLAND DEBUT 31.05.2000,
against Ukraine

When Gareth Barry played against Spain in 2007, it was his first international appearance in four years. Since then, Barry played in **20 consecutive matches** for his country and regularly plays under Fabio Capello. The Aston Villa midfielder grabbed his **first England goal** in 2008, to go with the ten caps he earned that same year.

ASHLEY YOUNG

International Friendly
Holland v England
Amsterdam ArenA – Holland
12.08.2009

BORN 09.07.1985, Stevenage
POSITION Winger
CLUB Aston Villa
CAPS 7
ENGLAND DEBUT 16.11.2007,
against Austria

A winger with **devastating pace**, Young sets up countless goals for his team-mates. At club level he's a **set-piece specialist**, taking care of free kicks and corners with assured accuracy. Still just 24 years of age, Young is showing **great potential** to be a real England star of the future.

STEVEN GERRARD

BORN 30.05.1980, Liverpool
POSITION Midfielder
CLUB Liverpool
CAPS 78
ENGLAND DEBUT 31.05.2000, against Ukraine

Steven Gerrard's **speed**, **strength** and **skill** on the ball make him one of the most talented midfielders around. The Liverpool captain was awarded the 2007 **Nationwide England Player of the Year** trophy two days before the Three Lions took on Switzerland in early 2008. Before the 2010 World Cup, Gerrard had taken his goal tally to an impressive 16 strikes in 78 games.

JAMES MILNER

International Friendly
England v Egypt
Wembley Stadium – London
03.03.2010

BORN 04.01.1986, Leeds
POSITION Midfielder
CLUB Aston Villa
CAPS 7
ENGLAND DEBUT 12.08.2009, against Holland

Comfortable playing in the centre of midfield or out on the wing, Milner is gifted both **physically** and **technically**. James holds the record for Under-21 appearances, having featured 46 times at that level. Turning 25 in January 2011, he will soon be reaching the peak of his **footballing powers**.

SHAUN WRIGHT-PHILLIPS

International Friendly
England v Egypt
Wembley Stadium – London
03.03.2010

BORN 25.10.1981, Greenwich
POSITION Midfielder
CLUB Manchester City
CAPS 30
ENGLAND DEBUT 18.08.2004, against Ukraine

Wright-Phillips is one of a few England stars to have **scored on his international debut** after scoring his first goal against Ukraine in 2004. As one of England's most **dangerous attacking** players, he made four victorious England appearances in 2008 and scored the **winning goal** in Fabio Capello's first match in charge.

STEWART DOWNING

International Friendly
England v Slovakia
Wembley Stadium – London
28.03.2009

BORN 22.07.1984, Middlesbrough
POSITION Winger
CLUB Aston Villa
CAPS 23
ENGLAND DEBUT 09.02.2005, against Holland

Having earned eight England Under-21 caps, Downing was called up for the senior squad to face Holland in 2005. Naturally left-footed and displaying **pace** and **top-class crossing** ability, Fabio Capello became the third successive manager to pick Downing for the England squad.

THEO WALCOTT

International Friendly
England v Egypt
Wembley Stadium – London
03.03.2010

BORN 16.03.1989, Stanmore
POSITION Midfielder
CLUB Arsenal
CAPS 9
ENGLAND DEBUT 30.05.2006, against Hungary

Theo Walcott became England's **youngest ever player** aged just 17 years and 75 days when he made his debut in 2006. Coming on for Michael Owen in his first match, Walcott beat Wayne Rooney's previous record as England's youngest cap.
Walcott was part of Capello's starting eleven for the 2010 World Cup Qualifier away to Croatia. It was here he became the youngest ever England player to **score a hat-trick**.

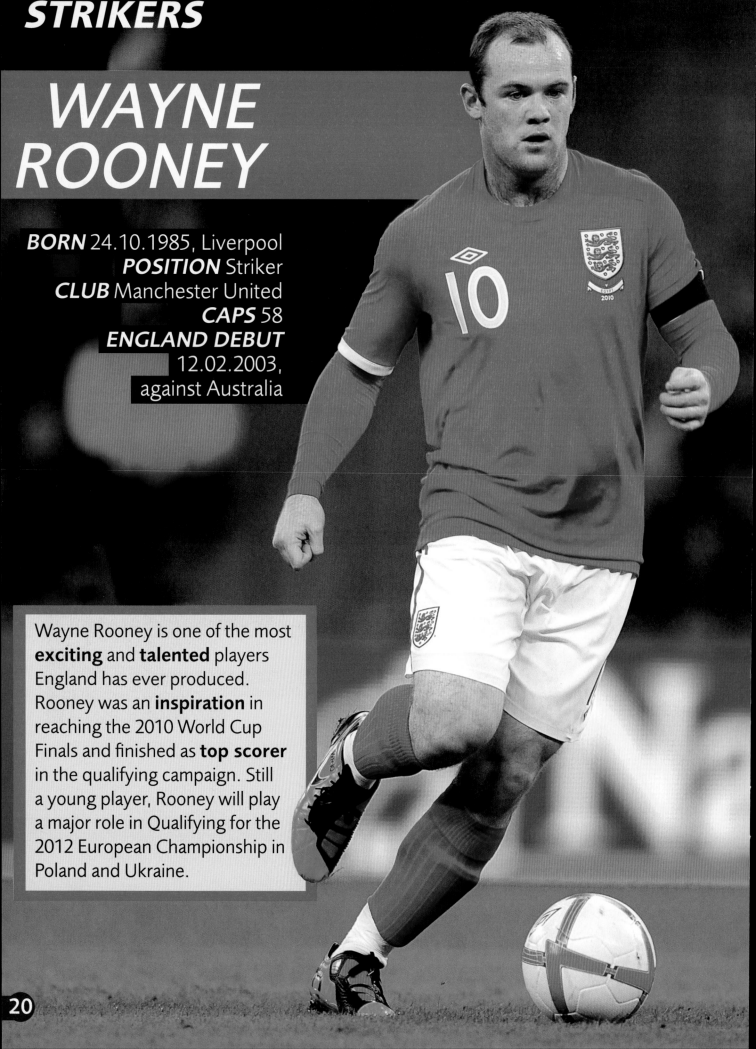

WAYNE ROONEY

BORN 24.10.1985, Liverpool
POSITION Striker
CLUB Manchester United
CAPS 58
ENGLAND DEBUT 12.02.2003, against Australia

Wayne Rooney is one of the most **exciting** and **talented** players England has ever produced. Rooney was an **inspiration** in reaching the 2010 World Cup Finals and finished as **top scorer** in the qualifying campaign. Still a young player, Rooney will play a major role in Qualifying for the 2012 European Championship in Poland and Ukraine.

PETER CROUCH

International Friendly
England v Egypt
Wembley Stadium – London
03.03.2010

BORN 30.01.1981, Macclesfield
POSITION Striker
CLUB Tottenham Hotspur
CAPS 37
ENGLAND DEBUT 31.05.2005,
against Colombia

Peter Crouch won his first cap during the USA Tour in May 2005. In 2008, Crouch switched clubs from Liverpool to FA Cup winners Portsmouth, and after an **impressive** spell was signed for Tottenham Hotspur by manager Harry Redknapp. Crouch's scoring record in his first 37 caps is an **outstanding** 20 goals.

JERMAIN DEFOE

International Friendly
England v Egypt
Wembley Stadium – London
03.03.2010

BORN 07.10.1982, Beckton
POSITION Striker
CLUB Tottenham Hotspur
CAPS 39
ENGLAND DEBUT 31.03.2004,
against Sweden

Defoe's **great form** at club level, for West Ham United, Portsmouth and Tottenham Hotspur, has propelled him into the international **spotlight**. A pacy striker with a natural eye for goal and **a powerful shot**, he has scored a brace on four different occasions for England.

CARLTON COLE

International Friendly
England v Egypt
Wembley Stadium – London
03.03.2010

BORN 12.11.1983, Croydon
POSITION Striker
CLUB West Ham United
CAPS 7
ENGLAND DEBUT 11.02.2009, against Spain

A Chelsea first-teamer at 19, Cole found his progression hindered and spent time on loan at Wolverhampton Wanderers and Aston Villa. In 2006 he signed for West Ham United and **flourished** under the guidance of former manager Gianfranco Zola. With an **impressive scoring** record at club level, it won't be long before he makes a real impact on the international stage.

EMILE HESKEY

International Friendly
England v Egypt
Wembley Stadium – London
03.03.2010

BORN 11.01.1978, Leicester
POSITION Striker
CLUB Aston Villa
CAPS 57
ENGLAND DEBUT 28.04.1999, against Hungary

Powerful, quick and physically imposing, Heskey is a **bulldozer** of a centre-forward. He made his first international appearance under Fabio Capello in a friendly against Czech Republic in August 2008. He had such an **impact** in that match that Capello called on him on four other occasions that year, all in World Cup Qualifiers.

Test your knowledge of England teams past and present in these action-packed games, puzzles and quizzes.
Will you be man of the match?

SPOT THE BALL

Can you guess where the ball is in the action photo below? Use the letters and numbers running vertically and horizontally along the grid to give your answer.

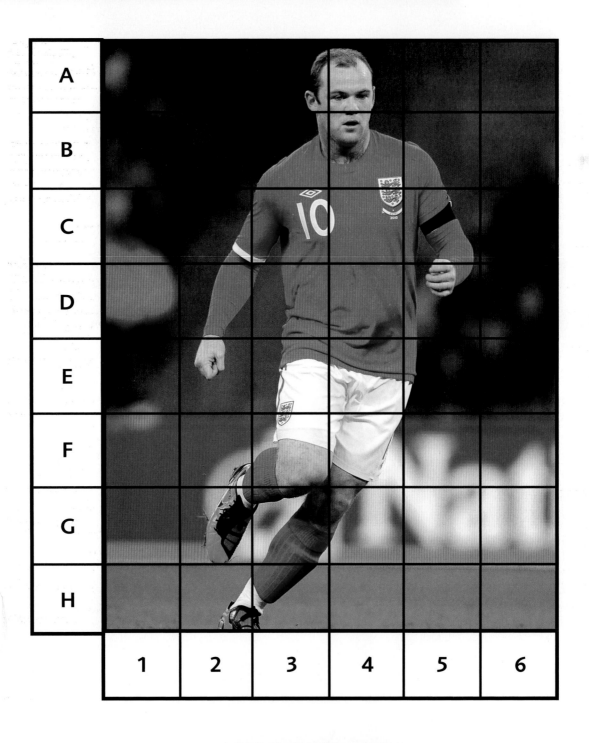

The ball is in square: ....

GUESS THE PLAYER

Can you identify which England players are in these blurry pictures?

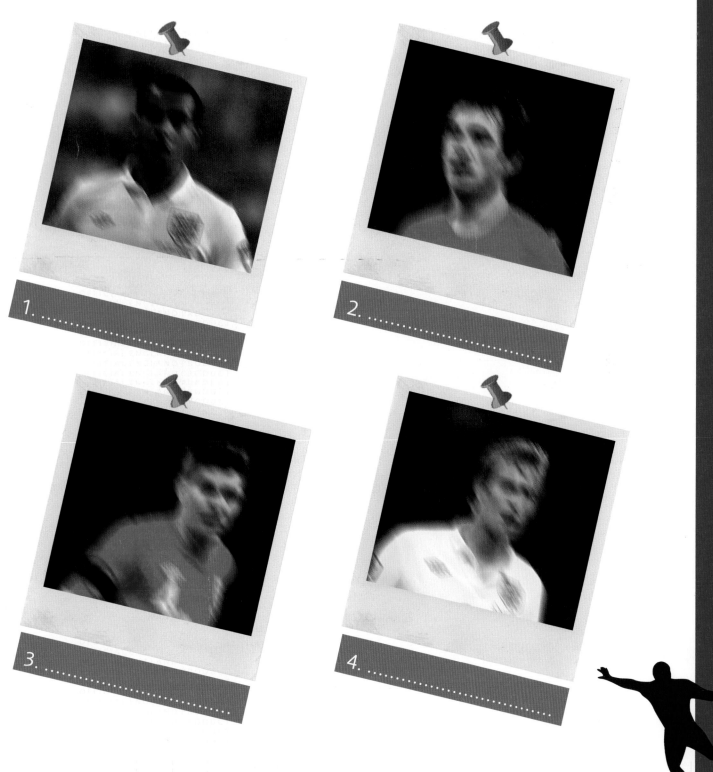

1. ....

2. ....

3. ....

4. ....

CREST CREATION

Famous throughout the world, the Three Lions badge is as recognisable as the flag of St. George itself. Using the Three Lions crest for inspiration, can you design a national badge worthy of being worn by the England team?

ENGLAND

PLAYER PERFECTION

Look at the grid below, only one of the passing options will result in a goal. Is it 1, 2 or 3?

Your pass will bounce off the angles like this: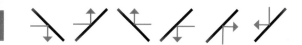

= GOAL!

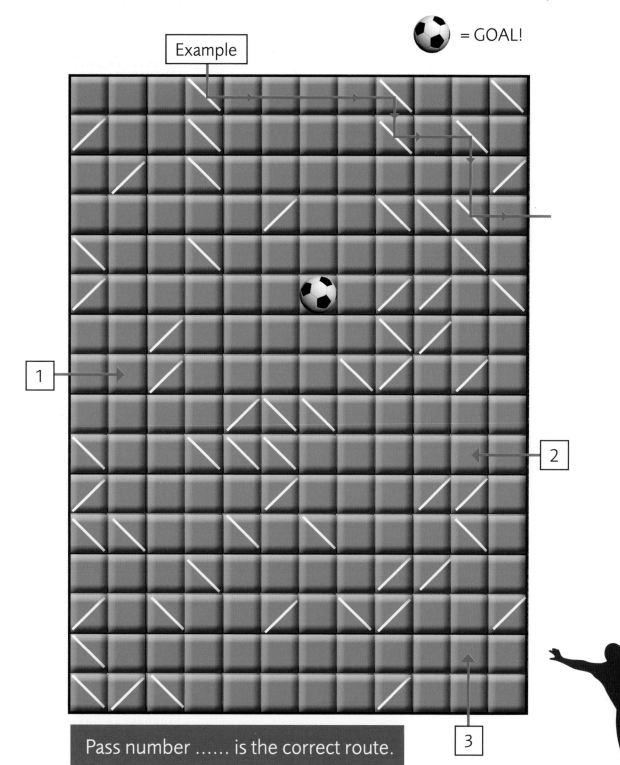

Pass number ...... is the correct route.

WORDSEARCH

Can you complete your own World Cup squad by finding all the player surnames below? You can search forwards, backwards and diagonally. Glory awaits!

There is also one name of an England World Cup hero in the wordsearch! Can you find it?

MOORE

COLE
CROUCH
FERDINAND
GERRARD
GREEN
LAMPARD
LENNON
ROONEY
TERRY

F	Y	E	N	O	O	R	L	G	J	U	L
Z	E	O	H	Y	H	G	A	A	J	J	D
U	K	R	R	C	E	I	M	C	N	M	U
C	O	R	D	R	U	B	P	L	O	D	J
Y	E	X	R	I	T	O	A	C	N	S	F
T	D	A	E	M	N	X	R	R	N	B	U
G	R	E	E	N	O	A	D	C	E	C	A
D	N	J	T	X	X	O	N	A	L	O	K
K	I	H	G	B	Y	E	R	D	P	L	E
L	F	F	J	A	H	S	W	E	S	E	Y
W	M	W	S	E	T	V	B	W	A	C	Z
Z	J	O	O	R	C	X	E	D	B	M	J

ENGLAND EXPERT

How much do you know about the England team?
Answer the questions below, then see how you scored.

1. Which player became England's youngest ever goal-scorer in Skopje?

2. Who was the first player to reach 100 caps for England?

3. Peter Crouch is England's tallest-ever player at 6'7". True or false?

4. Which player had the honour of scoring England's 500th goal at Wembley Stadium?

5. What is England's biggest ever win at Wembley Stadium?

6. After making his debut for England, Steven Gerrard didn't taste defeat with the national team for 21 matches. True or false?

1 ....

2 ....

3 ....

4 ....

5 ....

6 ....

29

MAGIC MOMENTS

So far in his career as a professional footballer, Wayne Rooney has proven he has the ability and focus to become one of the world's greatest players. Why is this picture so important in the history of the England striker?

This goal was important because it was:

....

In a long and illustrious career, David Beckham has scored many important goals for both club and country. Here he is celebrating scoring an equalising goal in stoppage time against Greece, on 6 October 2001. Why was this goal so important for England?

This goal was important because:

....

FOOTY CROSSWORD

It takes years of studying to master football, but a good knowledge of the beautiful game gives you a head start! See if you can complete this crossword by answering the clues below.

ACROSS

3. 2009-10 FA Cup Finalists, ... (10)
6. Chelsea defender, ... Cole (6)
7. Manchester City midfielder, Gareth ..... (5)
8. West Ham 'keeper, Robert ...... (5)

DOWN

1. Tottenham Hotspur striker, Jermain ...... (5)
2. Liverpool midfielder, Steven .... (7)
4. Chelsea captain, John ...... (5)
5. Losing Finalists in 2006 World Cup (6)

SPOT THE BALL

Guess where the ball is in the footy photo below. Use the letters and numbers running vertically and horizontally along the grid to give your answer.

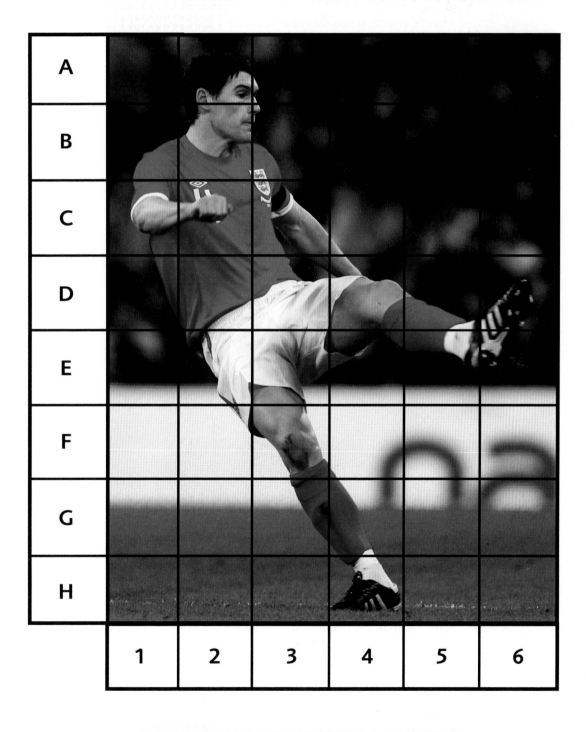

The ball is in: ....

DESIGN A KIT

There's no doubt about it, a professional footballer's ultimate dream is to represent their country. The white England home shirt with Three Lions on the crest is one of the most instantly recognisable and respected football shirts in the world!

Can you design the England team a shirt to wear on the world stage? Simply photocopy this page and away you go. If you have some friends over, why not all try designing a kit and then ask someone to judge the best one!

GUESS WHO?

Can you work out which player this is by looking at the photo and the clues?

Club side is Manchester City

First name has six letters

Second name has five letters

First name starts with G

Second name starts with B

Plays in midfield

Answer: ....

IDENTIFY THE PLAYERS

Can you work out who the mixed-up players are?

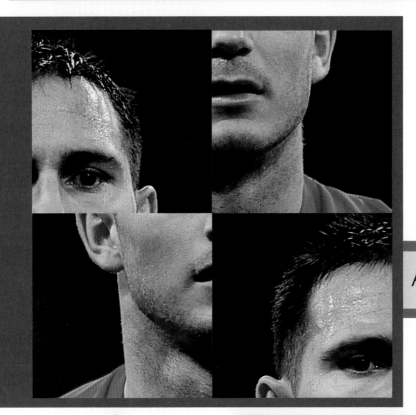

Answer: ....

Answer: ....

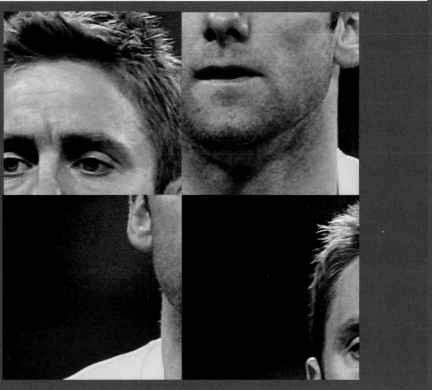

ENGLAND FANS

One great tradition of supporting your football team is to own a team scarf. These can be waved to show your support, or worn to keep warm in style.

Using the template below, try to design an awesome England scarf to be proud of.

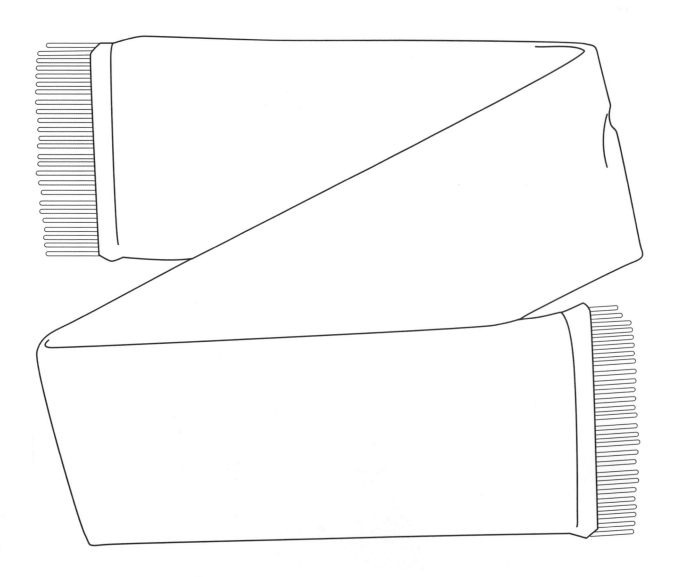

SPOT THE DIFFERENCE

Examine the football action scene below and see if you can find all five differences between the two pictures.

MAKE AN IMPRESSION

Have you ever wanted to be just like your England heroes? Here's your chance to replicate them while playing a fun game with your friends.

STEP 1: Choose a player that you want to do an impression of, but don't tell anyone who it is. It can be any player who has ever represented England.

STEP 2: Think about your chosen player.
• Does he have a special style of passing, shooting or heading?
• Does he have any on-field mannerisms?
• What is he famous for?
Try to come up with a few things you can act out as your chosen player.

TOP TIP:
What is your player famous for? Here Bobby Moore celebrates winning the World Cup. You could pretend to hold a trophy aloft.

TOP TIP:
What does your player do a lot during games?
As a goalkeeper, Robert Green dives around
making saves. Could you physically act like
your player?

STEP 3: Time to start doing your impressions. Your friend now has
to try to guess who you're doing an impression of – you're not
allowed to say anything or give them clues, they have to guess
the player based on your performance.

STEP 4: Take it in turns doing impressions and see
how many you can guess.

ANSWERS

PAGE 24

The Ball is in Square: H4

PAGE 25

1: Theo Walcott
2: Leighton Baines
3: Steven Gerrard
4: Peter Crouch

PAGE 27

Route 3 is the correct one.

PAGE 28

PAGE 29

1: Wayne Rooney
2: Billy Wright
3: True
4: Frank Lampard Junior
5: 9-0 against Luxembourg in 1982
6: True

PAGE 30

This goal was important because it was Rooney's first England goal.

PAGE 31

This goal was important because it ensured a dramatic qualification for the 2002 World Cup.

PAGE 32

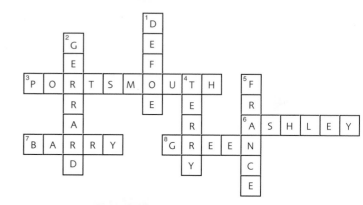

PAGE 33

The Ball is in Square: C4

PAGE 36

The player is Gareth Barry.

PAGE 37

1: Frank Lampard
2: Robert Green

PAGE 39

ENGLAND LEGENDS

Learn about the greatest players to ever represent England, from iconic World Cup-winners to present-day crowd pleasers. Who would make your all-time England dream team?

GOALKEEPERS

PETER SHILTON

BORN 18.09.1949, Leicester
POSITION Goalkeeper
CAPS 125
ENGLAND DEBUT 25.11.1970, against East Germany

One of the game's greatest goalkeepers, Shilton's ability was matched by his longevity – he played 1,390 times for 11 clubs during his career, finally calling it a day when he was 47 years old. He is England's most-capped player, making 125 appearances in a 20-year career.

GORDON BANKS

BORN 30.12.1937, Sheffield
POSITION Goalkeeper
CAPS 73
ENGLAND DEBUT 06.04.1963, against Scotland

When he kept out Pelé's goalbound header against Brazil in the 1970 World Cup, he became famous for the "save of the century". Banks is one of the finest goalkeepers to ever play the game. With brilliant positional sense, strong shot-stopping and cat-like reflexes, he was a goalkeeper that opposing strikers feared and respected equally.

DEFENDERS

BOBBY MOORE

BORN 12.04.1941, Barking
POSITION Defender
GOALS 2
CAPS 108
ENGLAND DEBUT 20.05.1962
against Peru

Leading by example both on and off the field, Bobby Moore is a football legend who led England to World Cup glory in 1966. A clinical tackler with pinpoint distribution, but never blessed with pace, his reading of the game meant he was rarely caught out and was always in the right place when his team needed him.
Statues of Sir Bobby Moore stand proudly outside Wembley Stadium and West Ham United's Boleyn Ground.

JOHN TERRY

BORN 07.12.1980, Barking
POSITION Defender
CAPS 59
GOALS 6
ENGLAND DEBUT 03.06.2003, against Serbia & Montenegro

One of the best defenders in the world, Terry is a fantastic player and with his club, Chelsea, he has experience of winning trophies. He relishes the on-field battle, and will put his body on the line to prevent his team conceding a goal. He is also a dangerous scorer from set-pieces.

RIO FERDINAND

BORN 07.11.78, Peckham
POSITION Defender
CAPS 76
GOALS 3
ENGLAND DEBUT 15.11.1997, against Cameroon

A born leader, Rio Ferdinand knows what's expected of him when he pulls on an England shirt. A quick thinker with a natural eye for a defence-splitting pass forward, he both prevents goals against his team and provides assistance to the attack.

JACK CHARLTON

BORN 08.05.1935, Ashington
POSITION Defender
CAPS 35
GOALS 6
ENGLAND DEBUT
10.04.1965, against Scotland

Jack Charlton was nearly 30 years old when he was first called up to play for England, but that made no difference to the confidence of this no-nonsense defender. He was a key player in the 1966 World Cup squad and was instrumental in winning trophies for his club, Leeds United.

BILLY WRIGHT

BORN 06.02.1924, Ironbridge
POSITION Defender
CAPS 105
GOALS 3
ENGLAND DEBUT 28.09.1946,
against Northern Ireland

William 'Billy' Wright was a legend for his club, Wolverhampton Wanderers, and his country, which he captained a record 90 times (a record shared with Bobby Moore). He was an inspiring defender who played without fear and drove his team forward.

GEORGE COHEN

BORN 22.10.1939, Kensington
POSITION Defender
CAPS 37
GOALS 0
ENGLAND DEBUT 06.05.1964,
against Uruguay

Cohen was a right-back with very good reading of the game. Were he playing today, his devastating speed and overlapping wing-play would still entertain the crowds at any modern football stadium.

JOHN BARNES

BORN 07.11.1963, Jamaica
POSITION Midfielder
CAPS 79
GOALS 11
ENGLAND DEBUT 28.05.1983, against Northern Ireland

Terrific pace and silky skills ensured Barnes' place in the hearts of the English fans. In the 1986 World Cup Quarter-final, he came on as a substitute and nearly stole the show from Argentina's match-winner, Diego Maradona.

KEVIN KEEGAN

BORN 14.02.1951, Armthorpe
POSITION Midfielder
CAPS 63
GOALS 21
ENGLAND DEBUT 15.11.1972, against Wales

An England record of a goal every three games tells you all you need to know about this exciting midfielder. Due to his bravery, speed and energy, he was later used as a support striker, creating goals for himself and his team.

49

PAUL GASCOIGNE

BORN 27.05.1967, Gateshead
POSITION Midfielder
CAPS 57
GOALS 10
ENGLAND DEBUT
14.09.1988,
against Denmark

A master of technique, 'Gazza' provided many brilliant moments on the football field. His ability on the ball allowed him to split defences with ease, and his flick and volley against Scotland in the 1996 European Championship is still talked about by fans today.

DAVID PLATT

BORN 10.06.1966, Chadderton
POSITION Midfielder
CAPS 62
GOALS 27
ENGLAND DEBUT 15.11.1989,
against Italy

An attacking midfielder with an impressive goals to games ratio, Platt was famous for his trademark volleys. He was an energetic presence in midfield and was England's most reliable and consistent player in the early 1990s.

BOBBY CHARLTON

BORN 11.10.1937, Ashington
POSITION Midfielder
CAPS 106
GOALS 49
ENGLAND DEBUT 19.04.1958
against Scotland

A survivor the Munich air crash tragedy, Charlton went on to win the European Cup with his club and the World Cup with his country. In fact, Alf Ramsey built the 1966 World Cup-winning squad around the strength of Charlton's midfield performances. He was famed for his long-range goals from the depths of midfield.

BRYAN ROBSON

BORN 11.01.1957, Chester-le-Street
POSITION Midfielder
CAPS 90
GOALS 26
ENGLAND DEBUT 06.02.1980,
against Republic of Ireland

Known as 'Captain Marvel', Robson was the finest England midfielder in the 1980s and 90s. He was considered to be a perfect example of a modern midfielder, thanks to his ability across the entire football pitch. Sir Bobby Robson said of him "He was three players in one – a tackler, a goal maker and a goal taker."

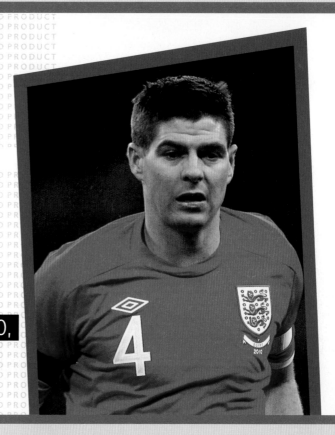

STEVEN GERRARD

BORN 30.05.1980, Liverpool
POSITION Midfielder
CAPS 78
GOALS 16
ENGLAND DEBUT 31.05.2000,
against Ukraine

Speed, strength and skill are all words associated with Steven Gerrard. He is one of the leading midfielders in the modern game; perfect in the tackle and lethal shooting from any range.

STANLEY MATTHEWS

BORN 01.02.1915, Stoke-On-Trent
POSITION Midfielder
CAPS 54
GOALS 11
ENGLAND DEBUT 29.09.1934, against Wales

Known as the 'Wizard of Dribble', Matthews mesmerised crowds with the ball seemingly glued to his feet. He was England's first Footballer of the Year in 1948 and was named European Footballer of the Year in 1956.

DAVID BECKHAM

BORN 02.05.1975, Leytonstone
POSITION Midfielder
CAPS 115
GOALS 17
ENGLAND DEBUT 01.09.1996, against Moldova

The most-capped outfield player in England's history, Beckham is famous for his accurate free-kicks and impeccable crosses from the right of midfield. His ability to pick out a pass to anywhere on the field has served him well playing in England, Spain, Italy and the United States of America.

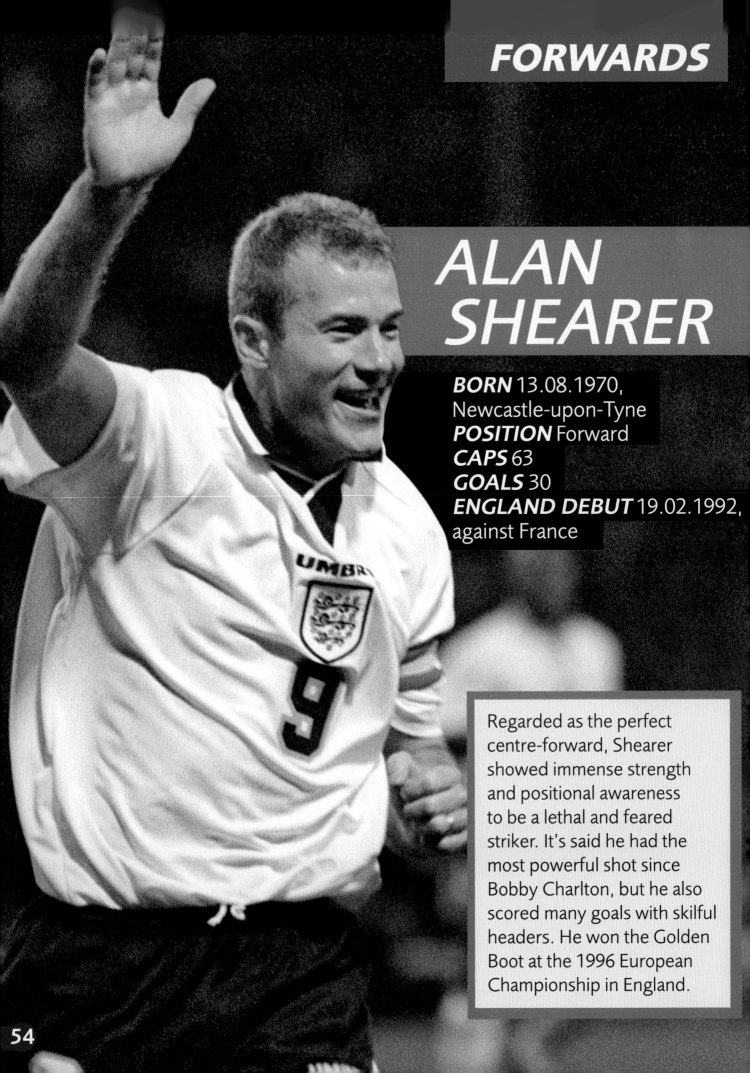

ALAN SHEARER

BORN 13.08.1970, Newcastle-upon-Tyne
POSITION Forward
CAPS 63
GOALS 30
ENGLAND DEBUT 19.02.1992, against France

Regarded as the perfect centre-forward, Shearer showed immense strength and positional awareness to be a lethal and feared striker. It's said he had the most powerful shot since Bobby Charlton, but he also scored many goals with skilful headers. He won the Golden Boot at the 1996 European Championship in England.

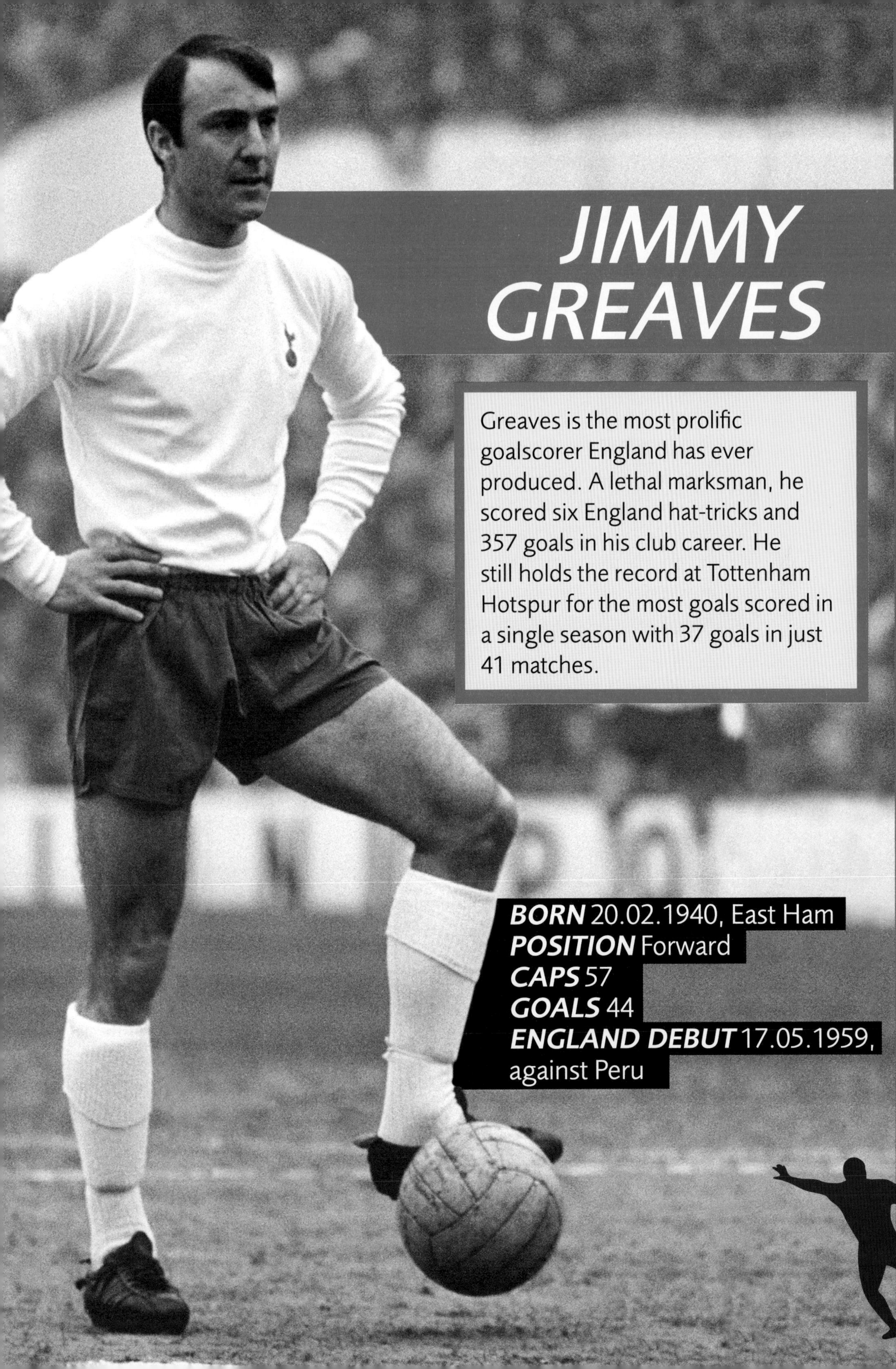

JIMMY GREAVES

Greaves is the most prolific goalscorer England has ever produced. A lethal marksman, he scored six England hat-tricks and 357 goals in his club career. He still holds the record at Tottenham Hotspur for the most goals scored in a single season with 37 goals in just 41 matches.

BORN 20.02.1940, East Ham
POSITION Forward
CAPS 57
GOALS 44
ENGLAND DEBUT 17.05.1959, against Peru

WAYNE ROONEY

BORN 24.10.1985, Liverpool
POSITION Forward
CAPS 58
GOALS 25
ENGLAND DEBUT 12.02.2003, against Australia

Put simply, Wayne Rooney was born to play football. He is a natural goal scorer and is on target to be England's all-time record scorer. However, his scoring ability isn't his only value to the team. He works hard across the whole pitch, and can often be found dribbling the ball out of defence and starting exciting counter-attacks.

GARY LINEKER

BORN 30.11.1960, Leicester
POSITION Forward
CAPS 80
GOALS 48
ENGLAND DEBUT 26.05.1984, against Scotland

One of the greatest forwards to put on an England shirt, Lineker scored 48 goals in 80 matches for his country – just one goal short of Bobby Charlton's record. He is the only ever English winner of the World Cup Golden Boot, after scoring six goals in the 1986 World Cup in Mexico.

GEOFF HURST

A natural winner, Geoff Hurst scored his famous World Cup Final hat-trick on only his eighth appearance for England. He had an unrivalled work ethic for a striker and boasted superb aerial ability, scoring many seemingly impossible goals with his head.

BORN 08.12.1941, Ashton-under-Lyne
POSITION Forward
CAPS 49
GOALS 24
ENGLAND DEBUT 23.02.1966, against West Germany

Now you know all about some of the greatest England players, it's time to decide your all-time England eleven! Fill in the team sheet below to complete your world-conquering team!

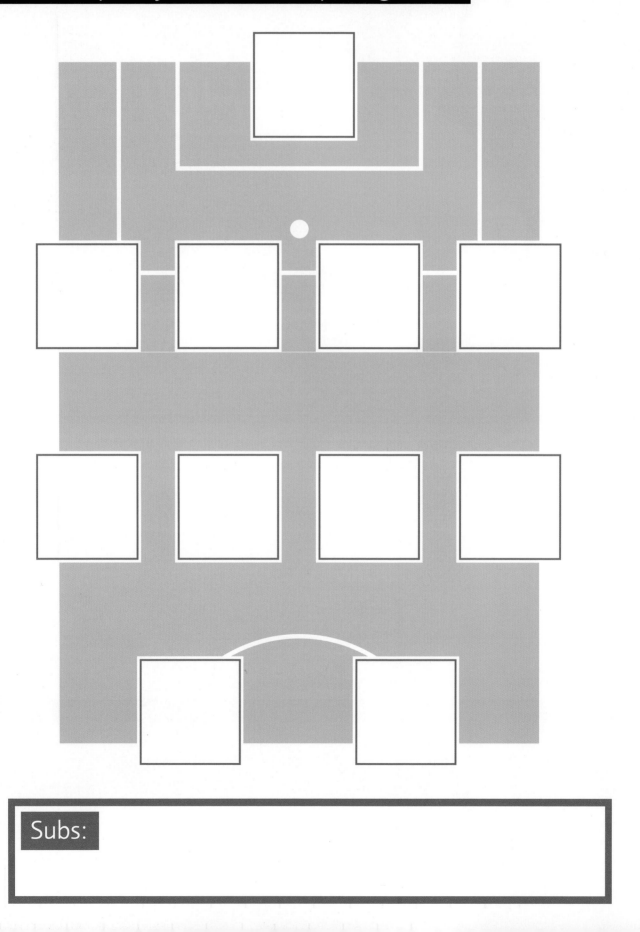

Subs:

COMPARE THE GREATS

The World Cup-winning team are remembered as some of the **greats of English football**. Find out how the current England squad compare with **the heroes of 1966.**

GOALKEEPERS

GORDON BANKS

VS

ROBERT GREEN

73	GAMES	9
0	GOALS	0
67%	WIN	67%
21%	DRAW	11%
12%	LOSE	22%

Robert Green has the same win percentage as the great Gordon Banks!

DEFENDERS

JACK CHARLTON

VS

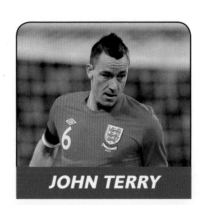

JOHN TERRY

35	GAMES	59
6	GOALS	6
71%	WIN	64%
23%	DRAW	20%
6%	LOSE	15%

BOBBY MOORE

VS

RIO FERDINAND

108	**GAMES**	76
2	**GOALS**	3
62%	**WIN**	58%
21%	**DRAW**	25%
17%	**LOSE**	17%

Rio needs to turn draws into wins to catch up with Bobby Moore.

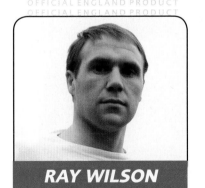

RAY WILSON

VS

ASHLEY COLE

63	**GAMES**	77
0	**GOALS**	0
57%	**WIN**	61%
25%	**DRAW**	23%
17%	**LOSE**	16%

ALAN BALL

VS

STEVEN GERRARD

72	GAMES	78
8	GOALS	16
62%	WIN	68%
26%	DRAW	21%
11%	LOSE	12%

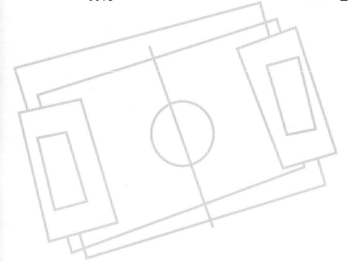

Although Ball's losing stats are better. Gerrard has scored more goals and has a higher win percentage for England.

Can Lampard catch Bobby Charlton's scoring record from midfield?

BOBBY CHARLTON

VS

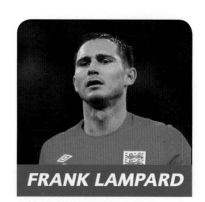

FRANK LAMPARD

106	GAMES	77
49	GOALS	20
57%	WIN	60%
23%	DRAW	21%
21%	LOSE	19%

NOBBY STILES

GARETH BARRY

VS

28	GAMES	36
1	GOALS	2
64%	WIN	64%
29%	DRAW	11%
7%	LOSE	25%

GEORGE COHEN

GLEN JOHNSON

VS

37	GAMES	20
0	GOALS	0
70%	WIN	70%
22%	DRAW	5%
8%	LOSE	25%

FORWARDS

ROGER HUNT

VS

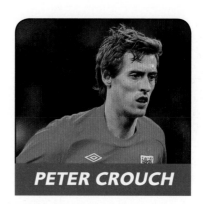

PETER CROUCH

34	GAMES	37
18	GOALS	20
74%	WIN	60%
21%	DRAW	21%
6%	LOSE	19%

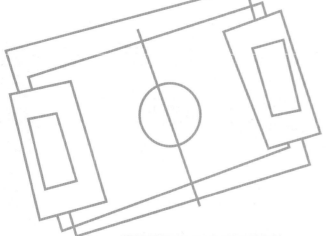

Rooney has already scored more than the 1966 Final's hat-trick hero Geoff Hurst, what can he go on to achieve?

GEOFF HURST

VS

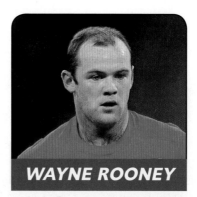

WAYNE ROONEY

49	GAMES	58
24	GOALS	25
63%	WIN	59%
24%	DRAW	21%
12%	LOSE	21%

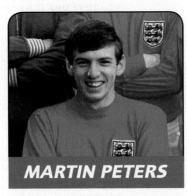 **VS**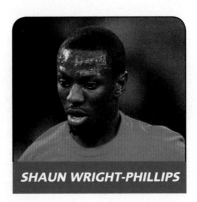

MARTIN PETERS   **SHAUN WRIGHT-PHILLIPS**

67	GAMES	30
20	GOALS	6
63%	WIN	57%
21%	DRAW	13%
16%	LOSE	30%

Martin Peters, scorer in the Final of 1966, currently holds better stats. But he'll be looking over his shoulder, as Wright-Phillips has become a major England force on the right wing.

HISTORY HIGHLIGHTS

- Defender Jack Charlton has the best winning percentage, winning 71% of his 35 England appearances.
- The highest career scorer to date is Bobby Charlton with 49 goals.
- If Wayne Rooney repeats what he has already achieved for England, he can become the all-time leading goalscorer.
- World Cup captain Bobby Moore had the same losing percentage as Rio Ferdinand – just 17%!

30 July 1966, Wembley Stadium – London Jack Charlton, Bobby Moore and Geoff Hurst celebrate winning the World Cup.

ICONIC ENGLAND

Few things evoke as much passion and pride as when the England football team produces one of those special moments that you'll remember forever. Check out some of the iconic footballing moments from the past 45 years of Team England.

It's been over 135 years since the England team took part in what was the first-ever official international football match. Even then, on a rainy November afternoon in 1872, some 4,000 people watched a 0-0 draw with Scotland unfold. In the years since, the interest and passion for the England football team has grown and grown, and playing for England is the proudest moment of a player's career.

1966 – WORLD CUP FINAL – BOBBY MOORE

30.07.1966
Bobby Moore celebrates winning the World Cup and holds the Jules Rimet trophy aloft for a crowded Wembley Stadium to see.

1966 – WORLD CUP FINAL – GEOFF HURST

30.07.1966

Geoff Hurst scores the fourth goal against West Germany to make the final score 4-2 in the dying seconds of the game. This goal prompted commentator Kenneth Wolstenholme to say "Some people are on the pitch! They think it's all over! It is now, it's four!"

2001 – WORLD CUP QUALIFIER – DAVID BECKHAM

06.10.2001

Seconds away from failing to qualify for the 2002 World Cup Finals, David Beckham scores a trademark free-kick to seal England's place in the competition.

1990 – WORLD CUP SEMI-FINAL – PAUL GASCOIGNE

04.07.1990

Paul Gascoigne can't hide his tears as England are denied a place in the Final after losing on penalties to West Germany. After receiving a yellow card during the game, Gascoigne would have missed the Final, had England won the dreaded penalty shootout.

1996 – EURO '96 SEMI-FINAL – STUART PEARCE

22.06.1996

Stuart Pearce screaming with pride after scoring his penalty in the Euro '96 Quarter-final, six years after famously missing his spot-kick against West Germany at the 1990 World Cup. His bravery in taking a penalty, and his reaction to scoring, is considered one of the most passionate displays ever seen in an England shirt.

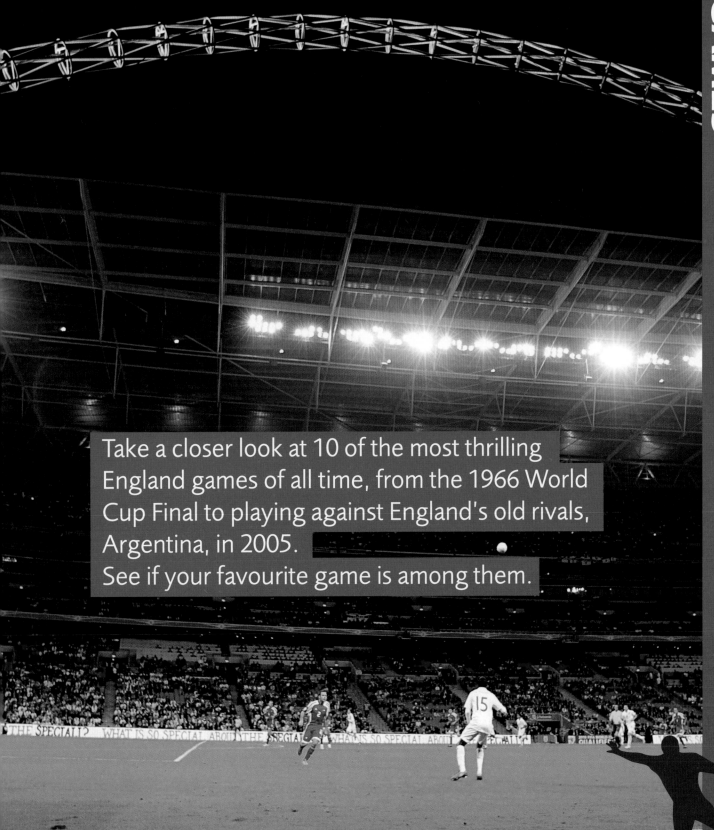

GREAT GAMES

Take a closer look at 10 of the most thrilling England games of all time, from the 1966 World Cup Final to playing against England's old rivals, Argentina, in 2005.
See if your favourite game is among them.

WORLD CUP 1966

THE OCCASION:
World Cup Semi-final, Wembley, 26 July 1966

WHO'S PLAYING?
England v Portugal

SCORE: England 2, Portugal 1

As the country began to dream of England's first World Cup Final, Alf Ramsey and his men were fully focused on the threat provided by Portugal in the Semi-finals. The Portuguese were a technically gifted team filled with plenty of class acts, including super strikers Eusébio and José Torres.

During a tight first-half, England enjoyed plenty of possession but failed to create many clear-cut chances, and Eusébio was looking dangerous in attack. With half an hour played, Bobby Charlton rattled the ball into the back of the net after Roger Hunt's shot rebounded back off the Portuguese 'keeper to give England a vital lead.

In the second half, the Three Lions continued to press forward but still defended stoutly, with Nobby Stiles marking dangerman Eusébio extremely tightly. With just over ten minutes of play remaining, Geoff Hurst latched onto a long ball from Stiles and held off the challenge of his marker before laying the ball back to Bobby Charlton. Without hesitation, Charlton slammed the ball into the corner of the goal with awesome power and gave England a two goal lead.

Eusébio fired home a penalty three minutes later to keep English nerves jangling, but the defence held strong and Alf Ramsey's men reached the Final with Charlton the hero.

England goalkeeper Gordon Banks punches the ball clear.

WORLD CUP 1966

THE OCCASION:
World Cup Final, Wembley, 30 July 1966

WHO'S PLAYING?
England v West Germany

SCORE: England 4, West Germany 2

Germany started off as slight favourites, so it was no surprise when they took the lead after just 12 minutes. But England were soon back in it, with Geoff Hurst heading home a free-kick from the England skipper Bobby Moore.
And it stayed at 1-1 until 12 minutes from the end.

Martin Peters then put England back into the lead, tapping home from close range. The Wembley crowd went mad but then disaster struck. Germany won a free-kick, the ball cannoned off the wall and fell to the German defender Wolfgang Weber, who slotted it past the England 'keeper Gordon Banks to make it 2-2.

When it came to extra-time it all became very controversial. A shot by Hurst hit the underside of the bar and bounced down. "But did it cross the goal line?" the referee asked the linesman. They had a brief chat and then the referee pointed towards the centre circle. Goal! England were 3-2 up.

This time, the Germans failed to come back. With the last kick of the game, Hurst scored and became the first player to score a hat-trick in a World Cup Final. England were World Champions.

England captain Bobby Moore holds the World Cup aloft as he is carried by his jubilant team-mates.

CAMEROON 1990

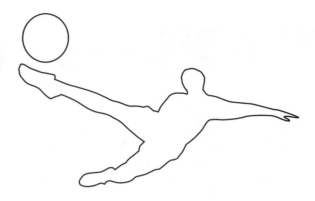

THE OCCASION:
World Cup Quarter-final, Naples, 1 July 1990

WHO'S PLAYING?
England v Cameroon

SCORE: England 3, Cameroon 2

David Platt scored the only goal of the first half, heading home a Stuart Pearce cross. But although Cameroon had plenty of chances to draw level, Peter Shilton and the rest of the England defence just about stood firm.

At the start of the second half, England finally cracked, with Paul Gascoigne fouling Cameroon star Roger Milla in the box. The resulting penalty levelled the score sheet at 1-1. England began to look a bit creaky and within five minutes of their first goal the Africans were ahead 2-1.

Things were not going to plan at all. The English midfield were being over-run and half the defence was limping. Time was ticking away. With seven minutes left, in a last ditch attempt to level the score, England hero Gary Lineker surged into the box but was sent flying. Penalty! Up stepped Lineker to make it 2-2 and take the game into extra-time.

It ended with a fantastic finish. Paul Gascoigne split the defence with a perfect pass, and as Lineker ran into the box, the Cameroon 'keeper ran out to meet him, resulting in another penalty for the Three Lions. Once again the team's hopes rested with Lineker. Will he blast it or place? Go right or left? Lineker went straight down the middle...but the 'keeper went to his right, resulting in a 3-2 win, which propelled England into the Semi-finals.

England's John Barnes on the attack.

SCOTLAND 1996

THE OCCASION:
European Championship Group Stage, Wembley, 15 June 1996

WHO'S PLAYING?
England v Scotland

SCORE: England 2, Scotland 0

As a frustrating first half for the Three Lions came to an end with the scores locked at 0-0, many England fans were concerned about their side's tournament chances. Scotland had battled well and enjoyed plenty of possession, defending stoutly and often out-numbering the English in midfield.

England manager Terry Venables brought on a young Jamie Redknapp at the beginning of the second half, and his accurate passing played a major role in England taking charge.

The first goal came after a surging right-flank run from Gary Neville, whose deep cross was finished off by the reliable head of Alan Shearer. Scotland refused to give

in and after 76 minutes they earned a penalty after a rough Tony Adams tackle on Gordon Durie. Gary McAllister stepped up to take the shot, but halfway through his run up, the ball moved slightly on the penalty spot. He took the kick anyway, and David Seaman pulled off a fantastic save to maintain England's lead.

Just three minutes later, Gazza scored after flicking a Darren Anderton through-ball over his body and avoiding the challenge of Scottish defender Colin Hendry with his left foot. He then allowed the ball to drop, before catching it full on the volley with his right foot, beating goalkeeper Andy Goram's flailing dive to settle the match.

Paul Gascoigne celebrates his goal with Teddy Sheringham.

HOLLAND 1996

THE OCCASION:
European Championship Group Stage, Wembley, 18 June 1996

WHO'S PLAYING?
England v Holland

SCORE: England 4, Holland 1

It started with Alan Shearer blasting England ahead from the penalty spot after Paul Ince had been tripped. But it wasn't until the second half that England upped the tempo and began purring like a finely tuned engine.

England were beginning to play football worthy of their reputation as one of the world's best teams. Teddy Sheringham headed in the second goal from a Paul Gascoigne corner, but the best was yet to come.

Steve McManaman passed to Gascoigne, who skipped past a defender before passing the ball to Teddy Sheringham. Everyone thought Teddy was going to shoot, but instead he slid the ball across the box to Shearer, who smashed home his second goal of the game.

Darren Anderton's long shot was saved by the Dutch 'keeper Edwin Van Der Sar, but it squirmed free and Sheringham tucked home the rebound for 4-1.

Holland did get one back and that was enough to see them qualify for the next stage, knocking out Scotland in the process.

England's Paul Gascoigne in action against Holland.

GERMANY 1996

THE OCCASION:
European Championship Semi-final, Wembley, 26 June 1996

WHO'S PLAYING?
England v Germany

SCORE: England 1, Germany 1 (5-6 on penalties)

At the start, England got off to an absolute flyer when Alan Shearer headed home a near-post corner after just two minutes. It looked like it was going downhill after that…Germany equalised just over ten minutes later. But both teams held steady and there were no more goals, causing the game to go into extra-time and then Golden Goals, with the next team to score the winners.

First, Darren Anderton was inches away with a shot that flew across the face of the goal. Then moments later, Stefan Kuntz scored for Germany at the other end. The 76,000 people who had crammed into Wembley looked at the referee; the referee looked at his linesman; the linesman looked back at him. "No goal," said the man in black. The game was still on!

Suddenly Shearer found himself out on the right wing. Racing up the pitch to the German goal, he passed to Paul Gascoigne, who slid in dramatically...but missed the ball. The referee blew the whistle, signalling that dreaded occasion: penalties.

Incredibly, England scored the first five but, unfortunately, so did Germany. So up stepped Gareth Southgate. As the nation watched, he ran forward and hit it too close to the 'keeper. Cue Andreas Möller, who stroked the ball past David Seaman and put Germany into the Final.

England Captain Tony Adams clashes with Germany's Andreas Möller during the Euro '96 Semi-final at Wembley Stadium.

ARGENTINA 1998

ENGLAND

Glenn Hoddle's England team had negotiated the first round group after a pair of 2-0 victories over Tunisia and Colombia, and were ready to up their game against the highly-rated Argentine side. The South Americans could boast the likes of Ariel Ortega and Gabriel Batistuta in their ranks, and were one of the most dangerous teams left in the competition.

The game was played at a ferocious pace, with both teams crunching into tackles and determined to attack. Argentina struck first when, after just five minutes, Batistuta was felled in the area by David Seaman and the referee awarded a penalty. 'Batigol' dusted himself down to convert the penalty and take the early lead for his team. Five minutes later, Michael Owen was brought down in the box as the Argentine defence struggled to cope with his pace, and Alan Shearer stepped up to the spot to equalise with typical conviction.

England were now equal and Owen and Shearer could smell blood. After 15 minutes, Owen picked up the ball near the halfway line and began a blistering run through the heart of the South Americans. Gliding past challenges, the teenager arrived in the area and drilled a deadly accurate strike into the roof of the net to give England the lead.

The Argentinians then began to dominate and, after plenty of possession, equalised on the stroke of half-time after Javier Zanetti finished off a clever free-kick. In the second half the game changed, when David Beckham was sent off by referee Kim Milton Nielsen for retaliating to Diego Simeone's wind-up tactics.

The brave ten lions held on for extra-time and penalties and could even have won the game, but Sol Campbell's header was ruled out. As Paul Ince and David Batty failed from the spot in the shoot-out, England crashed out of another World Cup. But they could return home with their heads held high after a memorable match and a courageous performance.

David Beckham gets sent off in the game against Argentina.

GERMANY 2001

THE OCCASION:
World Cup Qualifier, Munich, 1 September 2001

WHO'S PLAYING?
England v Germany

SCORE: England 5, Germany 1

Germany had a six point lead at the top of the qualifying group for the 2002 World Cup and only one team were certain to go through.

Six minutes into the game, Carsten Jancker gave Germany the lead. But then England went on an incredible scoring spree. First, Michael Owen smashed home a tremendous half-volley and then Steven Gerrard went one better, with an absolute screamer from 30 yards out. The England fans at the ground went barmy!

Michael Owen celebrates scoring against Germany.

As half-time approached, England's confidence was soaring and it wasn't long into the second half when Owen took advantage of the flagging German defence to bag his second goal, after a knock down from strike partner Emile Heskey. Owen then completed his hat-trick as his electric pace left Germany reeling and he launched the ball into the back of the net to make it 4-1.

The final blow to Germany was dealt by Emile Heskey, who scored to make it 5-1. It was Germany's worst defeat since they lost 6-0 to Austria in 1930.

THE OCCASION:
European Championship Quarter-final, Lisbon, 24 June 2004

WHO'S PLAYING?
England v Portugal

SCORE: England 2, Portugal 2 (5-6 on penalties)

ENGLAND

It started unbelievably well for England. David James launched a huge goal kick, which Michael Owen controlled brilliantly before flicking it over the 'keeper into the back of the net. England were one up with just three minutes on the clock.

Portugal didn't equalise straight away, and England managed to hold on until seven minutes from the final whistle. But then, Portuguese substitute Helder Postiga sneaked past the England defence to head the ball home. This meant extra-time, but only after Sol Campbell had a perfectly good goal ruled out right on the final whistle. Instead it was Portugal who went ahead, this time through a fantastic strike by Rui Costa after 110 minutes.

England were down but not out yet. Displaying his technical supremacy, Frank Lampard stabbed the ball home from close range to keep England's hopes alive and send the match into penalties.

However, David Beckham slipped as he ran up to take the first kick and sent it over the bar. At 5-5, Portuguese goalkeeper Ricardo saved well from Darius Vassell and then cruelly rubbed England's noses in it by stepping up to slot home the winner himself.

Portugal defeats England 6-5 on penalties in the Quarter-finals of Euro 2004.

ARGENTINA 2005

THE OCCASION:
International Friendly, Geneva, 12 November 2005

WHO'S PLAYING?
England v Argentina

SCORE: England 3, Argentina 2

In David Beckham's 50th match as captain, England met their old rivals Argentina in Switzerland. The South Americans came to Europe with a very high reputation, and they soon showed exactly why, playing some superb one and two touch football, dominating the midfield and looking dangerous going forward. For once, a friendly match was taken extremely seriously, possibly because the neutral venue enhanced the atmosphere and the game, likening it to a World Cup contest.

Inspired by their outstanding playmaker Juan Roman Riquelme and exciting winger Maxi Rodriguez, Argentina took control of the game and took the lead through Hernan Crespo after 35 minutes. But Wayne Rooney grabbed an equaliser before half-time to level the scores and keep England in the game.

In the second half, defender Walter Samuel popped up with a header to regain the lead for Argentina and England looked to have just fallen short. Sven-Göran Eriksson threw caution to the wind and brought on Peter Crouch for defender Luke Young and went for broke. The Argentinian back-four struggled to contain the Liverpool striker as he dragged them out of position and won everything in the air. The ensuing confusion was tailor-made for Michael Owen, who snapped up a brace of goals in the final minutes to turn the match on its head and give the players and supporters an inspiring victory.

England's Michael Owen celebrates scoring the winning goal as Argentina goalkeeper Roberto Abbondanzieri lies despairingly on the floor.

81

CROATIA 2009

THE OCCASION:
World Cup Qualifier, Wembley Stadium, 9 September 2009

WHO'S PLAYING?
England v Croatia

SCORE: England 5, Croatia 1

Needing a draw to get the one point that they needed, England went one better and sealed World Cup qualification with an emphatic 5-1 win in front of a packed Wembley Stadium.

Showing their nerves of steel, England took control of the game from kick-off. After just six minutes, Aaron Lennon was tripped in the penalty area by Croatia defender Josip Simunic. With set-piece pro Frank Lampard stepping up to take the penalty it was celebrations all round as England took an early 1-0 lead.

Lennon was again involved for the second goal, as he stood up an inviting cross that Steven Gerrard unleashed into the corner of the goal. England went in for the half-time break at 2-0.

In the opening moments of the second half, Croatia had more threat and decisiveness about their play and carved out a few chances, but

England defended solidly and didn't concede. At 59 minutes, Glen Johnson galloped down the right wing and crossed the ball to a waiting Frank Lampard, who calmly headed England 3-0 ahead. Just seven minutes later it was 4-0 to England as Gerrard scored his second from a Wayne Rooney cross.

Despite scoring soon after, through an Eduardo goal, England sealed the win after Rooney pounced on a fluffed back-pass by Croatian defender Ivica Krizanac, leaving him with the easiest goal of the evening. Final score England 5, Croatia 1.

In front of 87,319 home fans, England had banished recent memories of playing Croatia and qualified for the 2010 World Cup Finals in South Africa in emphatic style.

Devastated Croatian fans watch on as Gerrard scores his first goal of England's 5-1 demolition of Croatia.

EXCELLENT EIGHT

In qualifying for the 2010 World Cup Finals, Fabio Capello's England team won eight competitive matches in a row, a feat that has only happened three times since the Second World War. The last winning sequence as good as that was between October 2005 and June 2006. With Sven-Göran Eriksson at the helm, England won eight in a row before being held to a 2-2 draw by Sweden in the 2006 World Cup Group Stage.

Joe Cole skillfully scores one of his goals from close range to propel England to victory.

Two goals from midfielder Joe Cole sealed a positive start to England's qualifying campaign.

Croatia 1-4 England, 10.09.2008

Colour in this picture of Theo Walcott.

England banish recent bad memories and thrash Croatia on their home turf, thanks to a goal from Wayne Rooney and a hat-trick from Theo Walcott!

England 5-1 Kazakhstan, 11.10.2008

The first home game of England's qualifying campaign doesn't disappoint. The fans inside Wembley Stadium witness a five-goal thriller from a dominant England team. Goals from Rio Ferdinand, Jermain Defoe and two from Wayne Rooney add to a Kazakhstan own goal.

Belarus 1-3 England, 15.10.2008

Wayne Rooney slots home to complete a satisfying away win.

On the road, England once again look good while beating Belarus. Steven Gerrard opens the scoring before Wayne Rooney scores his second brace in successive games.

England 2-1 Ukraine, 01.04.2009

England returned to Wembley Stadium to meet a tough Ukraine side. With the score at 1-1, through goals from Peter Crouch and Andriy Shevchenko, John Terry scores the winning goal with just five minutes left on the clock.

Kazakhstan 0-4 England, 06.06.2009

England dominate on Kazakhstan's home soil through goals from Gareth Barry, Emile Heskey, a scorcher from Wayne Rooney and a penalty from Frank Lampard.

Colour in this picture of Frank Lampard.

87

England 6-0 Andorra, 10.06.2009

A six-goal stunner from the England team is their best competitive result for nearly ten years, since beating Luxembourg 6-0 in the qualifying stages for the 2000 European Championship. The goals were scored by Wayne Rooney (2), Jermain Defoe (2), Frank Lampard and Peter Crouch.

England 5-1 Croatia, 09.09.2009

Stamping their authority on qualifying Group 6 and showing their intent to the watching world, England seal qualification for the 2010 World Cup Finals with their eighth win in a row. Frank Lampard and Steven Gerrard scored two goals each before Wayne Rooney added a fifth.

Steven Gerrard leaps to head one of his two goals in front of an ecstatic Wembley Stadium. The goal helped seal England's World Cup place.

POLAND – UKRAINE
2012 EUROPEAN CHAMPIONSHIP

The 2012 European Championship is being hosted by neighbouring countries Poland and Ukraine. Create a record of England's campaign to reach the tournament.

Now approaching its 14th tournament, the European Championship began in the summer of 1960 and takes place every four years. England have never won the tournament and have had mixed results. They did however reach the Semi-finals in Italy at the 1968 Championship and again when they hosted the tournament in 1996.

The 1996 European Championship was remembered for the drama of its penalty shootouts. With Terry Venables in charge and England scoring almost at will, England won 2-0 against Scotland and 4-1 against Holland before meeting old rivals Germany at the Semi-final stage. Despite going a goal ahead through the star of the tournament, Alan Shearer, England eventually bowed out on penalties after an intense period of extra-time.

The 2000 European Championship in Belgium and Holland is worth remembering because England beat Germany for the first time in a competitive match since the 1966 World Cup Final, though they were ultimately eliminated in the First Round. The 2004 European Championship headed to Portugal and England unveiled a secret weapon – an 18 year old Wayne Rooney. Rooney lit up the tournament and helped England reach the Quarter-final, where they faced host nation Portugal. Unfortunately, Rooney picked up an injury and had to be substituted, and England went on to again be knocked-out on penalties.

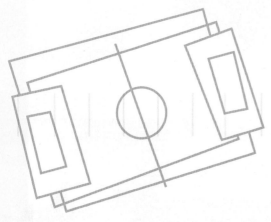

Wayne Rooney's injury changed the momentum of the 2004 European Championship Quarter-final.

EUROPEAN CHAMPIONSHIP PERFORMANCES

YEAR	HOST	ENGLAND'S PERFORMANCE	WINNERS
1960	France	Did not enter	USSR
1964	Spain	Did not qualify	Spain
1968	Italy	Semi-finals	Italy
1972	Belgium	Quarter-finals	West Germany
1976	Yugoslavia	Did not qualify	Czechoslovakia
1980	Italy	Round 1	West Germany
1984	France	Did not qualify	France
1988	West Germany	Round 1	Holland
1992	Sweden	Round 1	Denmark
1996	England	Semi-finals	Germany
2000	Belgium & Holland	Round 1	France
2004	Portugal	Quarter-finals	Greece
2008	Austria & Switzerland	Did not qualify	Spain

Colour in this picture of Lampard, Rooney and Carrick.

Keep a record of England's progress throughout their Euro 2012 qualifying campaign by filling in all the match facts and stats.

England v Bulgaria, 03.09.2010
Result: ....
Scorers: ....
Man of the match: ....
My match report: ....
....
....
....
....
....
....
....
....

Switzerland v England, 07.09.2010
Result: ....
Scorers: ....
Man of the match: ....
My match report: ....
....
....
....
....
....
....
....
....

England v Montenegro, 12.10.2010
Result: ....
Scorers: ....
Man of the match: ....
My match report: ....
....
....
....
....
....
....
....
....

Wales v England, 26.03.2011
Result: ....
Scorers: ....
Man of the match: ....
My match report: ....
....
....
....
....
....
....
....

England v Switzerland, 04.06.2011
Result: ....
Scorers: ....
Man of the match: ....
My match report: ....
....
....
....
....
....
....
....
....

Bulgaria v England, 02.09.2011
Result: ....
Scorers: ....
Man of the match: ....
My match report: ....
....
....
....
....
....
....
....
....

England v Wales, 06.09.2011
Result: ....
Scorers: ....
Man of the match: ....
My match report: ....
....
....
....
....
....
....
....
....

Montenegro v England, 07.10.2011
Result: ....
Scorers: ....
Man of the match: ....
My match report: ....
....
....
....
....
....
....
....
....